Maisie and Dot

And Other Stories from a Preschool Teacher

Anisa MacLean

NOTE TO READERS: Certain names and characteristics have been changed throughout the work, regardless of whether such changes are specifically identified.

Published by Anisa MacLean 2021

ISBN: 978-0-473-58158-9

For my sister, Delaram. Thank you for making me an aunt.

Contents

Introduction

Maisie and Dot is a collection of stories about some of the more memorable children which I taught and/or encountered during my time as a preschool teacher.

Preface

In my early twenties I went through an insomniac phase. At the time, I naively attributed my sleepless nights to watching too much Stranger Things on Netflix before bed with my now husband. Be that as it may, I also had quiet anxieties about our trans-national romance. I persistently thought he was going to leave me and go back to his old life and family across the globe at any given moment. In my equally idealistic and conservative Iranian thinking, I desperately needed a ring, or it wasn't serious. My insomnia got the better of me when he returned home to Nashville for Thanksgiving and I self-destructively convinced myself he wasn't coming back.

At this point in my life, the only thing keeping me sane was my role at Itty Bitties Preschool. A quaint family-home-turned-childcare-centre, Itty Bitties oozed warmth and bliss. I can still feel what it was like to walk into Itty Bitties off the quiet residential road and be embraced by a flavoursome concoction of loud laughter, bold colours, and the sweet smell of freshly baked chocolate-chip cookies. The teaching team (myself included) were a mishmash of various cultures and backgrounds. What linked us together was our commitment to the children. Teaching kept me moving. Being present with the children propelled me forward and helped me escape my personal anxieties which uninvitedly entered my thoughts every night at witching hour.

To help cure my sleeplessness, my doctor gave me some generic sleeping pills. Ironically, I remember feeling more alert after taking them. This led onto being prescribed something the doctor jokingly referred to as a 'horse tranquilliser'. When the horse tranquilliser didn't tranquillise me, I was referred to a community therapist on five free government-subsidised sessions (thank God for New Zealand's healthcare!). Like all good therapists, we didn't just talk about my current sleeplessness, but we also unearthed my dismal childhood of growing up in a home filled with anxiety in deeply political Iran. I learnt a lot about myself during those five sessions, sitting on the brown leather couch with the puppy-patterned tissue box always within arm's reach, thanks to my therapist's ability to mind-read then give it to me straight. Almost everything the therapist uttered resulted for me in a light bulb moment, the one most enlightening for this collection of stories being:

"And that is why you're a preschool teacher, Anisa. You have subconsciously chosen this career for two reasons. One, to empower your students at a time in their lives during which they may feel most powerless and two, as an attempt at redoing your own childhood for the sake of the wounded little girl within."

Maisie and Dot

Every now and then my boss would ask me to cover for an absent teacher at their second preschool of the same name. It was there, at the 'other' Itty Bitties, that I met Maisie and Dot.

Maisie immediately caught my attention. She reminded me of the chubby little girl, Olive I think her name was, from the iconic movie, Little Miss Sunshine. Like Olive, Maisie wore large peach-coloured, round-framed glasses, though Maisie's had a Jessie (the cowgirl from the Toy Story series) pattern. These further magnified Maisie's already curious owl-like eyes. She had a slight gap between her two front teeth and wore far too many sparkly hairclips in her pig-tail hairstyle — which always seemed to come undone from Maisie and her friends' endless chasing games.

I only had to watch Maisie for a minute to notice a little boy, much younger than the rest of the children at the preschool, always following Maisie's tail, his chunky thighs doing the classic toddler trot. His frantic yet short steps resulted in a trot-fall, trot-fall sequence until he reached his beloved sister. As it turns out, Maisie's brother was supposed to be in the nursery, not in the preschool with Maisie. He was a mere one-and-a-half years old, or as mothers like to say, eighteen months. However, each time Maisie's mum tried to drop him off at the nursery, separated from his Maisie, he would scream melodramatically in protest, often violently throwing himself against the ground to prove a point. He was so adamant to be with his beloved sister that he literally would not stop howling at the ground until he was back with her.

"He's only little..." Maisie would sweetly explain to the adults in her little brother's defence. In the end, it was simply easier to give in and allow him to transition to the preschool much earlier than intended than to keep him unhappy in the nursery with his peer group.

Maisie didn't mind having her little brother with her in the big room. In fact, I noticed she had the patience of a saint. For example, she'd hardly flinch when her little brother innocently continued his drawing from his paper across and onto hers. Actions that would inflame even the calmest child never bothered her. Instead, she'd simply shrug her shoulders and remind everyone that he was 'only little'.

Since I worked at the 'other' Itty Bitties sporadically, I often struggled to remember all of the children's names — except for Maisie's whose name I easily remembered.

One sunny afternoon, I watched as Maisie speedily crawled from one side of the playground to the other, pretending to be the ‘cat’ in her and her friends’ ‘Mums and Dads’ game. Her little brother was not far behind. With his arms swinging by his sides, he persevered through his trot-fall, trot-fall pattern in hope of catching up to his big sister. His snug black t-shirt, with the words ‘Little Brother’ on the front had ridden up, revealing his rounded belly. I couldn't help but imagine he was running for cake.

All of a sudden, he lost his balance and fell over just inches away from reaching Maisie. Naturally, he began to wail. Noticing the familiar cry, Maisie immediately turned around, broke out of her cat character, and started comforting her baby brother by placing her right arm awkwardly around his neck and using her left hand to stroke his face.

“Thank you for helping, Maisie,” I said once I had reached the pair. “What’s your little brother’s name, again?” I asked, kneeling down beside them.

“Dot,” she replied.

“What?”

“Dot,” she repeated.

“Sorry Maisie, can you say that again?” I couldn't quite understand what she was saying.

“Dot.”

“Dot?”

“Yes, Dot, Dotty. His name is Dot,” she explained, clearly

frustrated by her new teacher's incompetence. Then, “Well, sometimes daddy calls him Dotty Potty…” she tried again. “It’s SCOTT. She’s saying SCOTT,” an older child snapped in my face.

And that is how ‘Maisie and Scott’ came to be ‘Maisie and Dot’ in my heart — and of course, the inspiration for this wee compilation of stories on children.

Jojo

When Jojo first started at our preschool, she had just turned two. Her busy working mother had organised her entire enrolment with our office lady over the phone. This is because Grandma, who took care of her when Jojo's mother was engrossed in hitting her target at a downtown jewellery store, spoke little to no English. Grandma was a no-nonsense 60-something lady-boss from Shanghai. Before we had even opened the front door to the preschool, Grandma had transferred Jojo and her tiny red backpack, (containing her blankie, goat's milk and eczema cream) from her arms into ours without even crossing the threshold. Grandma meant business; she was always in a hurry, and she clearly valued her time.

"Take off, too hot outside," she'd say sternly, pointing to Jojo's fluffy leopard vest, or the opposite: "Put on she go outside, too cold!" raising her fists to her ears, making sure we understood what she meant.

At pick-up time, Grandma would always say the same thing. "She was okay," she'd declare more as a statement than a question. We would always respond warmly by giving her the rundown on Jojo's day. Grandma would smile and nod in acknowledgement before quickly moving past us to retrieve her precious grandchild.

We, the four teachers of Itty Bitties Preschool, very quickly fell in love with little Jojo. Some children just have that effect on you. Straight away, they claim a cosy nook of your heart, set out their favourite blankie and start a lifelong picnic with their best-loved toys. Plus, it did help that Jojo was uber-cute. She was an animated child. Even though Jojo had severe eczema across her body which caused her to itch at her flaky skin all day long, she never failed to grin from ear to ear. When Jojo was not having her nappy changed, eating her dairy-free food or taking her midday nap, she was enthusiastically engaged in chasing the other children around the preschool, her straight black bob bouncing from side to side. She moved with utter self-confidence believing herself a key member of everyone's crew.

In my naive attempt to communicate with Jojo, I started greeting her with the limited Mandarin I knew. "Nǐ hǎo," I'd wave to her upon arrival. "Nǐ hǎo, Jojo!" I'd call to her in the playground and "Nǐ hǎo sweetheart," I'd say when she first opened her tiny eyes after her midday sleep.

Before long, as children's communication skills naturally do, Jojo's English vocabulary boomed. In fact, she loved speaking English so much that her new favourite game was to point at different objects and people around the room and proudly name them in English. Jojo was especially fond of her peers and quickly learnt the names of all of our children.

One afternoon, I was holding Jojo in my arms when she spontaneously began naming the people in the photographs on our 'Our Teachers' wall display.
"Ashley," said Jojo with a smile.
"Hannah," she pronounced proudly.
"Victoria," she continued, emphasising the 't'.
Then, when she reached my photograph, a short and sure: "Nǐ hǎo".

A few weeks later, I joined little Jojo at the outside mud kitchen.
She was heavily absorbed in stirring gooey mud in an old metal pot when I audaciously asked her: "What are you cooking, Jojo? Are you making dumplings?" She ignored my question and carried on mixing her concoction.
So, I continued. "Do you like noodles?"
No reply.
"How about rice? Do you like rice?" I emphasised. Jojo stopped stirring the mud and turned to look me straight

in the eyes. Then, in perfectly clear English and with absolute self-assurance she declared: “I. Like. Pies.”

Lifa and Akiko met one another whilst backpacking in India. Both in their early twenties, Lifa, a party-boy welder from Tel Aviv, Israel, and Akiko (or, as her mother called her, Aki), a shy country girl from Kanagawa, Japan had come to India 'to find themselves'. To their pleasant surprise, what they had actually found was each other.

One hot and humid evening, days before Akiko's flight back to Japan, Lifa asked Aki to be his wife over a bowl of spicy hummus. "I don't care where we live, as long as I'm with you. Together we can conquer the world!" he had said.

A year later, Akiko gave birth to their first child. They named him 'Oz' meaning 'strength' in Hebrew. Lifa told me that, when Aki fell pregnant, they became adamant on raising their child multilingually — more than anything, Lifa's mother had stressed that their union, and moving to Japan, wouldn't equate to losing their mother tongue and heritage. So, Lifa spoke to Oz-kun[1] in Hebrew and Aki spoke to him in Japanese and since they themselves

[1] Kun is often attached to the end of Japanese boys' names as a term of endearment.

communicated with each other in English, Oz-kun was naturally exposed.

Three years later, I met their charming little family whilst teaching English as a Second Language (ESOL) in a group of preschools in rural Japan.

One Saturday morning, I had stumbled upon a quaint French bakery, which I later found to be run by a Québécois, Olivier, and his Japanese wife Hiromi, on one of my many no-destination bike rides through the picturesque countryside. Imagine field after field of greenery spotted with slouched elderly tending to their eggplants and tomatoes. Hugo et Leó stood out to me, as it was not common to see foreigners let alone 'foreign' stores in rural Japan. The prospect of biting into hard bread (most of the bread in Japan is soft like cake) propelled me to stop.

Inside, at the one communal table in the middle of the narrow shop sat Aki, a petite young woman with her straight black hair loosely tied in a bun above her head. She was sitting cross-legged on her stool in a pair of bright purple genie pants. Next to her was Lifa, a rather slender young man with kind brown eyes and strikingly thick facial hair. Across the table from his parents and facing away from me, sat little Oz-kun. As I took my first steps inside, he swung around and looked me directly in the eyes. Oz-kun's face was round, his features were dark, but his eyes were two delicate almonds identical to his mother's. In the middle of the table sat one half-eaten *pain au chocolat*.

We became instant friends. Suddenly, I found myself transitioning from eating dinner alone in my tiny studio apartment to spending my evenings cosied up under the kotatsu[2] in their larger living room with Lifa and Oz-kun by my side, waiting for Akiko to bring us food. One evening, as the three of us patiently waited for our home-cooked meal of coconut dhal (you couldn't get more international than this family), Lifa pointed out Oz-kun's new drawings from preschool, which had been carefully taped to their living room wall. I immediately praised Oz-kun on his artwork and asked about his drawings. Oz-kun, who had remained relatively silent until the age of four, but had recently found his voice, swiftly replied: "Oh, that's a picture of me in our KHouse, that's me eating yoghuRt and that's me helping okāsan[3] making KHummus."

With each new heavily pronounced word, my eyes (and Lifa's smile) widened. It was the first time in my life that I was hearing a mid-sentence accent change, let alone one coming from a four-year-old. From Lifa's proud smile and

[2] A kotatsu is a low table with a heater attached underneath.

[3] Okāsan is Japanese for 'mum'.

nod I could tell such multilingual pronunciation had become commonplace in their home. I will never forget this occasion, and to this day, I cannot eat yoghuRt or KHummus without adding Middle Eastern zest to my pronunciation of the words.

Oliver

That memory of Oz-kun reminds me of an interaction I recently had with my nephew, Oliver. Ollie is three years old. His mother is my older sister, a dark-haired and beautiful Persian through and through. His father is Andrew Banks, a typical pale-skinned European bloke. I may be biased but Ollie turned out a dangerously delicious nugget of caramel toffee.

Fortunately for the both of us, Ollie recently began attending Itty Bitties too. The other day, I was sitting beside Ollie as he very carefully organised the plastic animals in order of largest to smallest (I've always thought him slightly OCD — I can say that because he's my nephew). When I got bored of observing him, I asked an unnecessary question, the answer of which I already knew, as adults in the presence of little children often find themselves doing unconsciously.

"What's that, Ollie?" I asked, pointing to the lion.

"That's a lion," Ollie replied without looking up.

He continued his orderly work.

"What's that?" I proceeded, pointing at the hippo.

"That's a hippo," Ollie said, squeezing his blonde monobrow into a slight frown.

I took his reaction as a cue to tweaking my questioning style.

"Is that a lizard?" I tricked, pointing to a snail.

"No, khaleh (auntie) Anisa, that's a halazoon (snail) and it has a SHELL!" barked bilingual Ollie, scrunching his pronounced Persian nose.

Jasper, Milo and Levi

Justin was in charge of drop-offs. Every Monday, Wednesday, and Friday morning, he and his two sons, Jasper (4) and Milo (2) arrived at Itty Bitties' front entrance, at precisely eight o'clock.

Jasper and Milo were polar opposites. Jasper was tall and scrawny with jet-black straight hair, and he was obsessed with construction vehicles. To say that he lived and breathed them would be an understatement. Jasper knew facts about heavy machinery that I bet even their drivers didn't know! He arrived at preschool with his feet halfway out of his shoes, ready to dive into the sandpit. I am confident that nothing made Jasper happier than a game of imaginary roadworks.

Side note: Jasper was so obsessed with construction that the only way to get him to go to the toilet was to make a game out of it. He was the 'project manager' and 'getting the wees out' was his project.

Milo on the other hand, was short and plump with fluffy thick brown curls. Milo's favourite thing to do at preschool was to play in the 'family corner' with the baby dolls and 'the girls'.

The girls, a group of BFF four-year-olds, simply adored Milo and took sweet care of him both during their play and with everyday tasks (like washing hands before food) around the preschool. It was easy to understand their attraction towards Milo as he was crazy cute just like a miniature poodle. Milo and the girls played dress-ups, sang top hit songs they'd heard on their parents' car radios, danced ballet, and cared for the baby dolls.

If I close my eyes, I can picture two-year-old Milo now. He is wearing an Elsa dress, his hair is wild, he is standing behind a dolly stroller, looking down at the half-dressed baby doll inside and ironically sharing his fondness of its cuteness with his girlfriends, whispering: "Aww, cute!"

Jasper and Milo arrived at preschool ready to play. As I mentioned before, Jasper's shoes were normally already half off upon arrival. Justin, on the other hand, was never ready to say goodbye. Instead, he lingered for what seemed an hour, insisting to read to his boys even if he was already late for work.

"How about a story? You know you want a story!" he'd push. Sometimes, the boys obliged — especially if the story in question was on princesses or roadworks. However, on this one occasion, I recall the boys completely ignoring their father's pleas for a story and doing what children do best: simply running off. This left Justin standing awkwardly in the middle of the classroom. "One last huggle, boys?" Justin called. "Boys?"

Nothing, the boys were out of sight and out of earshot. "Ah, I better go then, I guess…" Justin muttered to himself. This is when Levi, perhaps our most boisterous four-and-three-quarters-year-old, carefully walked up to Justin and tapped him on the leg.

"You could read me a story if you like?" he stated politely, his big blue eyes twinkling with hope. Now, it's important to mention that Levi's father had tragically died in a motorbike accident in Casablanca just as Levi's mother, Nora had found out that she was pregnant with him. In an attempt to beat her heartache, Nora had fled as far away as geographically possible from the scene of her beloved's death and started afresh in New Zealand. Here, she had singlehandedly fabricated a new life for her and her baby boy away from the judgement of her so-called family and friends. This meant working Monday–Friday with little Levi in childcare from sunrise to sunset. Nora knew her son was desperate for her time and attention, but she couldn't risk losing her job, especially with the current COVID-economy. When Levi had turned four, Nora braved the discomfort and told him the truth about his father's absence. Nowadays, Levi often spoke to us about his father, telling us how 'strong and fast' he was and how he was now always watching him and his mum ‘from the clouds’ and at other times ‘from the moon’.

Justin, though a little stunned by Levi’s proposition, agreed with enthusiasm. The odd pair walked over to our bookshelf where Levi chose a bright red book with a blue dinosaur on the front. As Justin sat down on the sofa, Levi took him off guard again by boldly settling himself onto Justin's lap.

And that, is the story of how Justin ended up reading Levi a captivating tale about underpants-loving dinosaurs whilst subconsciously filling both of their emotional cups before the workday had even begun.

These days, every time Justin hugs his boys goodbye, he intentionally saves an embrace for Levi, too.

Geeta and I

Geeta's parents didn't like her taking off her shoes. It was a protection mechanism. In fact, Geeta's mother, Bahnaz once told me that each day after Geeta's father brought her home from preschool, she would ask her daughter to stand in her undergarments so that she could give her a 'complete check-over' in case of a bump or a bruise.

"I need to make sure everything is okay with her," Bahnaz had genuinely explained. Unfortunately for her parents, Geeta loved playing in the sandpit. This meant half the sandpit would go home with Geeta everyday through her tightly velcroed shoes. She was a sweet and obedient child. She knew the importance of listening to her parents, as deeply ingrained in her through her Pakistani values.

In many ways, little Geeta reminded me of myself as a little girl growing up in Iran. I had been raised to always respect my elders (which we would NEVER address by first name — I remember being totally flabbergasted when I heard children calling grown men and woman by their FIRST NAMES once we arrived in New Zealand) and to be wholly obedient to my father, then my mother. Like Geeta, I too had memorised the 'rules'. At least, Geeta's warning to keep her shoes on at all times was arguably logical. My recurring warning from my mother, however, was not…until it was.

Apparently as a young child, I was prone to occasionally overeating and uncontrollably vomiting up my food — you only have to sample Persian food once to understand my fondness of it — you just can't stop! Weeks before my 7th birthday when Iranian children begin primary school, my mother had started warning me to hold back my new and white school uniform hijab[4], in order to prevent staining, if I were ever to vomit at school. So, I began my big school adventure with my mother's warning buzzing in my tiny ears. As the great foreseer of misfortune, my dear mother had still packed me my favourite *ghormehsabzi* stew (which I overate time and time again), for my first school day's lunch.

Ghormehsabzi is an extremely popular and flavoursome Iranian beef and kidney bean stew loaded with a bunch of greens like spinach, parsley, fenugreek and cilantro. Visually however, it looks like green gloop with floating mysterious chunks of brown and maroon.

By now, you must have guessed where this story is headed… It was the period after lunch when my stomach

---

[4] A large piece of cloth that is wrapped around the head and upper body leaving only the face exposed.

started to do somersaults. I excused myself from the classroom and sprinted down the hallway towards the bathrooms.

"Hold back your hijab, hold back your hijab," my subconscious screamed at me. Unfortunately, that is when my two left feet got the better of me and I threw up mid-fall. Of course, I landed in my vomit, hijab and all. I shamefully returned to class with a face full of tears. My teacher took one look at me and my green front before asking the caretaker to send me home. I was placed in the back seat of a traditional yellow taxi feeling like an exile. The entire journey home, my eyes bulged in fear as I dreaded my mother's reaction. When the taxi driver turned into our street, my heart skipped a beat. My mother, who had been notified by the school, was waiting in her black chador[5] at the front entrance of our apartment complex. I could see her right fingers in motion as she cracked her knuckles—something she often did in times of nervousness.

"I'm so sorry I forgot to hold back my hija…" I blurted out before the taxi driver had fully opened my door. My mother

[5] A long, loose cloak worn over other garments by Muslim women, especially in Iran and South Asia, consisting of a semicircular piece of cloth draped over the hair and shoulders to cover the body while leaving the face uncovered or partially concealed.

took one look at me and my grossly stained attire before responding with the most high-pitched howl of laughter.

The only other time I've heard my mother laugh like that was at the 'fly incident'. Flash-forward one year, I was now eight years old and performing as the fly narrator in a bug production at my primary school in New Zealand. My costume consisted of dark pantyhose (no shoes) under a black dress with my entire face smothered in black face paint. A teacher said something to the audience and the room quietened. When the curtain fully opened, I buzzed onto the wooden stage. I started my performance by simultaneously flapping my hands while circling the stage. I can still remember feeling super nervous at mispronouncing my lines in English — the excruciating foreign language I initially felt forced upon me by my parents' move to New Zealand. You've got this, eight-year-old me, you've got this!

Some twenty years later, I still blame my teachers for not foreseeing the obvious outcome of pantyhose on polished wood, for on my second circling of the stage, my foot skidded on the wooden flooring, causing me to dramatically fall face-first just inches away from tumbling off the stage. Like a scalded cat, I scrambled to my feet and forcefully regained my composure. Tears filled my eyes as I looked towards my family for reassurance, who I knew were seated at the front. Reassurance, my ass! For that is the exact moment when I witnessed it again. My mother's entire body was hunched over. Her hands were holding her stomach and she was howling. 'Twas the return of the Ghormehsabzi Laugh.

Shiva and Ethan

Itty Bitties was renowned in the neighbourhood for its daily cooked lunches. We knew this from the countless parent praises we received each day. It seemed, parents appreciated their children eating hot lunches (especially during the colder months of the year) and — who are we kidding — this is probably the real reason, delighted in removing the stress of making packed lunches themselves. So, when COVID-19 reared its monstrous head, as a precautionary measure, the hot lunches stopped, and parents were asked to start packing lunches for their children.

"Yuck!" said Ethan, four going on fourteen, pointing to Shiva's lunch on Monday. "What's that green stuff?"

"*Kookoo sabzi*," replied Shiva, a sweet little Iranian girl who had been with us for less than a week.

"*Kookoo sabzi*?" Ethan mimicked, screwing up his freckled nose. "What's that?"

"It's like a frittata with herbs and spinach. Would you like some?" Shiva offered sweetly. "I have extra today."

"Me eat slimy spinach?" Ethan hooted. "No way!" The children giggled in support of him.

"That's not kind, Ethan!" I interjected.

On Tuesday, Shiva's mother had sent her with *fesenjoon* — brown and sticky in appearance.

"Ugh, what is that?" asked Ethan with his mouth full.

"It's chicken stew with walnuts and pomegranate." Shiva replied, this time with less confidence.

"Icky stew!" jeered Ethan biting into his marmite and cheese sandwich.

"Bummygranite?" said Ethan's best friend, Quinn, whose round face resembled an oversized beetroot. The children burst into laughter.

"That is ENOUGH!" I snapped before ringing our Tibetan Singing Bowl aka our 'calm bell'. The children fell silent. I thought about moving Ethan to a different table, then simply shrugged off my disappointment.

On Wednesday, Shiva's lunchbox was filled to the brim with *aash*, a thick soup made with leafy greens, wheat noodles and kidney beans. The soup was garnished with swirls of *kashk* (sour yoghurt) and minty fried onions. Its familiar aroma made my mouth water.

"Gross, gross, gross!" chanted Ethan and Quinn bumping their fists on the table.

"Gross, gross, gross!" the other children repeated.

"This behaviour needs to stop right NOW!" I declared before banishing the boys to separate tables.

On Thursday, Shiva's lunchbox held a large flatbread, two short and fat minced kebabs, and one round chargrilled tomato.

"Yuck!" whispered Ethan. "That looks like p…"

"Ethan!" I narrowed my eyes, "Do you need to go to the toilet?" His cheeks flushed red.

Quinn roared with laughter.

Amber leaned towards Shiva. "That bread looks yummy, May I have a taste?"

Shiva broke off a piece and handed it over. Before I could stop the exchange, Amber said: "Mmm, that's yum!"

"We're not supposed to be sharing food, girls," I gently reminded them before smiling a little smile of triumph for Shiva's instant win.

At pick-up time that afternoon, I pulled Shiva's mother aside. I told her what had been happening at lunchtimes and I assured her I was keeping an eye on the situation.

On Friday, Shiva and her mother arrived at preschool at lunchtime, much later than usual. Shiva's mother was holding a big silver pot in her arms.

"This is *sholezard*," said Shiva. "It's a traditional pudding made with rice, saffron and cinnamon. It's my favourite and my mother has made enough for everyone to taste!" Her voice shook a little bit.

“Saff who?” mumbled Ethan. “Still yuck!” he breathed in Quinn’s ear loud enough for all of us to hear. My eyeballs nearly jumped out of their sockets. I could not believe the audacity of that boy! I remember thinking there was absolutely no way that I could turn down Shiva and her mother’s generous offer after that comment.

“That is so kind, Ayma, thank you!” I said to Shiva's mother before taking the pot from her. I can easily recall the sweet fragrance of that *sholezard* wafting through my nostrils and flirting with my stomach as I divided the yellow pudding amongst small bowls for the children.

“I don’t want any!” said Ethan when I placed his portion in front of him.

“Why don’t you just try it, young man?” Ayma gently insisted.

Ethan looked around the room at his peers. Everyone was enjoying their share. Even Quinn was licking his fingers! Slowly, slowly, so the other children wouldn’t notice, I pushed the bowl of *sholezard* closer to Ethan who dramatically scrunched his nose, probably to save face, before slowly dipping the tip of his little finger into the sticky pudding and licking it. Straightaway, I could tell that he liked it, for his eyes looked the same way mine did every time I tasted my mother’s Persian cooking. Ethan’s eyes were beaming. Quickly, I handed him a teaspoon. To my surprise, he used it to gobble down every last bit of the *sholezard* in his bowl. Suddenly, Shiva looked over our way.

"Ethan, did you just…?"

"That was the best thing I've ever tasted!" he said. Ayma smiled the reassuring I-told-you! smile at her daughter, perfected by every mother on the planet. "I'm so happy you liked it, Ethan!" Shiva grinned. "I did!" he said. "Now let's go outside and play!"

Chase

Do you remember the once viral YouTube video 'Charlie Bit My Finger'? At Itty Bitties we had our own biting Charlie — except our fun-sized crocodile was called Chase and his biting wasn't considered adorable by his witnesses. Not one bit(e).

Chase looked twice his age. He was four (I'll do the math for you), but I swear — he looked eight! He was tall, beefy and surprisingly strong for a young child. He had a kind face, but his eyes screamed mischief.

Chase was what is considered a 'late talker' in Early Childhood Education (ECE). At the age of four, he was still mostly communicating non-verbally or in poorly pronounced single words. So, we attributed his biting behaviour to his lack of communication; where other children used their words in times of conflict, Chase used his incisors. Chase's biting became such a problem that we teachers started taking turns shadowing him. This is because, as we found out the hard way, he could pounce at any moment!

Every time Chase added a new victim to his casualty list, we were professionally obliged to notify both parties' parents. Surprisingly, the bitee's parents usually took the news well. I think, they were secretly happy it wasn't their child doing the biting. Chase's parents, however, were absolutely mortified.

Chase came from a family of working professionals. His mother was a gynaecologist with her own private practice, his father was an orthodontist and both of his grandparents on his father's side were internationally renowned surgeons. In other words, money was not a problem for this family. When we notified Chase's parents of his biting behaviour, Chase's father always apologised with such sincerity, I half-expected him to kneel and start begging at any given moment. Incidentally, in the year and a half that I taught Chase, his parents gifted us teachers bakery bread boxes, day spa vouchers, ceramic reusable cups, scented candles, fancy bottles of wine, and endless boxes of gourmet chocolate just 'because'.

Then, just as we decided to seek outside intervention for Chase's biting problem, it was as if he flipped a switch and became a completely different child altogether.

New Chase could not only talk, but he was talkative: "Come on!", "Let's play!", "Look at this!" and "WOW! What's that? What's this?" he'd say in absolute excitement, luring in his ex-victims. To our surprise, all of the children would willingly follow him! Ironically, Chase went from being feared and avoided to the most popular boy at preschool overnight!

What I admired about Chase's character was his openness to play with everyone. Chase wasn't choosy in his friendships — the same way he hadn't been choosy with his victims! He went from playing 'bad guys' with the boys (basically chasing each other in circles whilst riding bikes) to wearing Frozen dresses and dancing on the deck with the girls, all in the same hour.

In times of conflict, Chase became the first child to swiftly seek out a teacher and rat out his classmates' bad behaviour. I was so proud of him! Chase's newfound words seemed to be the beginning of the end of his biting behaviour, so we stopped shadowing him.

Then one day, after months of zero casualties, Chase struck again. His sitting duck was no other than my innocent nephew, Oliver.

Chase was happily playing by himself with the little yellow construction vehicles in the sandpit. He had created a wonderful work site with several holes and hills. Oliver, much like his two-year-old peers, was a self-proclaimed digger expert. Oliver entered the sandpit, saw the little yellow construction vehicles, and with Chase in his peripheral vision, he claimed the beloved Little Yellow

Digger for himself. Chase shrieked in despair; with no time for chit-chat, he pounced, and snatched the digger out of Oliver's hand, demonstrating his annoyance by sinking his teeth into Oliver's exposed shoulder. Now it was Oliver's turn to howl. Having witnessed the whole ordeal in what seemed like slow-motion, I picked up my nephew and began comforting him, the bite mark on his shoulder now filled with tiny blood droplets.

That evening, after months of good news, I informed Chase's father of the incident. The poor man's face turned as pale as chalk.

"I'm so sorry," he said looking down at his Calvin Klein trainers.

"It's okay! These things happen. They're children, it's normal, It's okay!" I tried reassuring him.

The next morning, we teachers got the biggest shock of our careers when we entered our staffroom. For there, on the small table where we huddled to eat our lunches, in all its glory sat a boxed DeLonghi La Specialista Maestro Pump Espresso Machine with a Post-it note on top: 'To my teachers. I'm so sorry. Love, Chase.'

Rest assured, I never drank a caffé from that glorious beast without sending a silent 'salute' to my darling Oliver.

Carter and Cooper

Carter and Cooper were identical twin brothers. They had short blonde hair and sweet yet equally mischievous faces sitting above their scrawny frames. Initially, I had difficulty telling them apart — it didn't help that their parents always dressed them exactly the same (can someone please explain the reasoning behind this?) I kept calling Carter Cooper and Cooper Carter, thus embarrassing myself and annoying them.

"I'm not Cooper!" Carter would say, scrunching his little nose and vice versa. Determined to tell the boys apart, I remember fixating on their faces looking for just one noticeable difference and finding that Cooper's eyes were slightly cross-eyed compared to his brother's.

Cooper and Carter, Carter and Cooper, to use the 'forbidden word' in ECE, were extremely naughty! However, as I'd come to learn through working as a preschool teacher, the naughty children were the most charming of all. So, I took great joy in quietly observing the troublesome twins.

Throughout the preschool day, the twins constantly drove us (and each other) bananas.
If they weren't grappling like Tom and Jerry, you'd find the brothers dangerously dangling from the money bars or

lifting solid objects like metal trikes and seeking validation with such proud statements as: "Watch me! I can lift this with one finger!" (whilst actually lifting with two hands) and "We're FOUR!"

And, although the boys' wrestling looked savage from an onlooker's perspective, the shared laughter between the two monkeys made it pretty clear that their intention was far from causing each other any harm. Funnily, Carter often unintentionally put his pants on backwards causing his drawstring cords to resemble a primate's tail.

At lunchtime, Cooper would ravenously eat everything in his lunchbox apart from their mother's homemade carrot muffin: "I don't like my muffin! I don't like my muffin! I don't like my muffin!" he'd repeatedly say until he was acknowledged. In contrast, Carter simply grazed at one or two items.

Come afternoon snack time, Cooper had nothing to eat (except for the dreaded muffin) whereas Carter's lunchbox was still filled to its brim. With his eyes on the prize, Cooper would inch his seat closer to Carter's. "I don't like my muffin!" he'd remind no one in particular, to which we teachers finally intervened and asked Carter if he was willing to share some of his leftover lunch with his brother. Without speaking a word, Carter would take his carrot muffin and drop it next to Cooper's neglected one.

My favourite time to eavesdrop on the twins was at the end of the day when their father came to collect them. The twin's father oozed importance. He had no hair, which made his dark-rimmed glasses the predominant feature in his appearance. He always carried a leather briefcase and he repeatedly dressed in a suit and tie combo despite the scorching hot weather. The juxtaposition between the twins and their father simply added to their comedic nature.
"Daddy!" the boys called out in unison running towards their father.
"Hi boys. How was your day?" he said as he knelt collecting the twins' belongings.
"Daddy, Carter broke Optimus Prime!"
"No, Cooper broke him!"
"I warned you boys to keep Mr. Prime at home."
"Carter broke Optimus Prime!" Cooper repeated.
"No, I didn't."
"Did too."
"Did not."
"Did!"
"That's enough!" their father interjected. "Unless you tell me the truth about what happened to Optimus Prime, you're not allowed back here."
The boys were silent as they carefully pondered their next move. They loved coming to preschool. It was their arena. This forced them to pull out all the stops. They looked at

each other then back at their poker-faced father who was waiting for their answer, then back at each other again. Cooper spoke first. “Tyler did it!” he declared with triumph, eyes gleaming.

Tyler was their teenage brother.

“Tyler? Tyler lives in Wellington!” said their father, clearly at a loss. He stood up, flung their identical Transformers backpacks over his shoulder and made for the exit. “Until you boys tell me the truth—,”

“Carter broke Optimus Pri—,”

“Did not!”

“Di—,” and they were out.

Tilly

This wouldn't be a genuine compilation of 'stories from a preschool teacher' without featuring the prevalent P-word in ECE. Tilly, just two, was distinctly petite, barely larger than an American Girl doll, her delicate features as cute as a newborn kitten. So, it was a big surprise for Tilly's parents when she sensibly unclasped her nappy, climbed on top of their adult-sized toilet (at preschool we have mini toilets which are much easier to conquer) and performed a triumphant wee!

"I DID A WEE!" Tilly had squealed from their bathroom, grinning from pigtail to pigtail. That night, Tilly's family held her a 'toilet party'. Her mum baked a lemon cheesecake and her dad rushed to The Warehouse to buy her a 3-pack set of Disney briefs. As it turned out, sweet Tilly was going to need a lot more than just three.

After one week of being nappy-free, Tilly started at Itty Bitties. She loved preschool immediately. Like a child let loose at a carnival, Tilly couldn't decide what to give her attention to first. She dashed from one side of the preschool to the other, dropping toys she had so eagerly pursued just seconds earlier only to move on to the next shiny item. During her first few weeks at preschool, Tilly was a busy bee as she excitedly flapped her tiny arms by her sides, swiftly buzzing between our upstairs room and downstairs playground continually seeking MORE FUN! Of course, amidst all of the fun the humble toilet was the last thing on Tilly's mind. So began 'The Poop Series' with the most memorable being the 'Playdough Incident'.

Every Monday morning, we made fresh playdough for the week. On this particular Monday, I was feeling extra creative and decided to make rainbow-coloured playdough with the children. I made plain playdough without any colouring first. Then, I divided the dough into similar sized chunks and dyed each chunk individually using powered dye. Eventually we had four chunks of playdough in the colours amber red, mustard yellow, sage green and sky blue, which within a nanosecond, the children refashioned into a single-blended brown. By the afternoon, the brown playdough was surprisingly in full swing with a good portion of the dough having been thrown on the floor. It was at this time that little Izzy innocently picked up what she assumed was a ball of playdough and proceeded to do what children do best: mutate its form.

Children make sandcastles only to destroy them as fast as possible. Mini muffins become flattened biscuits, and playdough balls remodel into playdough disks in children's tiny yet ruthless hands. As you can imagine, or maybe you shouldn't, Tilly's solid piece of poo underwent a big transformation between Izzy's palms; once a firm segment, now sticky gloop.

When Tilly's mum found out about the 'Playdough Incident', she was so embarrassed she baked us teachers an apology mud cake. 'The Poop Series' lasted six whole months before very regular Tilly — what was she eating…prunes? — was fully toilet trained. During those six months, we teachers ate so much apology baking that I'm willing to bet Tilly's brief collection grew at the same rate as our workpants shrunk.

Arthur

I once taught the grandson of a famous artist, except I didn't know Arthur's family history at the time. It was only recently, after an internet dive, that I came to learn of Arthur's legendary lineage. All I knew of Arthur's family for the duration I was his preschool teacher was what he had told me himself in his posh English accent, that his mother 'made beautiful earrings' and his father 'designed photocopiers'. Anyway, the humble aurora which Arthur's nuclear family carried everywhere they went, left me no reason to think any different.

In saying that, from the very first instant I laid eyes on Arthur, I sensed something spectacular about him and his character. To be fair, he was a very noticeable child. Arthur was taller than most three-year-olds. His lanky limbs were always dressed in bright clothing (of his own choosing), and he wore multiple hairclips in his soft, blonde, doll-like hair to make way for his curious green eyes.

Often, Arthur arrived at preschool with shapes and symbols (stars, hearts and the occasional medical plus sign) drawn on his cheeks and forehead with black eyeliner. "He asked for them!" Arthur's mum would dismiss with a kind smile. On dress-up days, where the other children turned up in identical Batman and Spiderman costumes, Arthur arrived sporting his creative ideas, modestly brought to life by his mother, my favourite being the Babybel cheese; literally two pieces of round cardboard painted red with the label 'Babybel' written across the middle, strapped together with rope which Arthur wore over the top of his shoulders.

"I love a good Babybel. As well as a good halloumi cheese," Arthur proudly repeated to literally every adult he encountered that day, his vigorous eyes widening a little further each time.

In fact, catching adults off-guard with his unconventional anecdotes was Arthur's superpower. By three years of age, the sort of conversations his peers were having had become too unimaginative for Arthur's level, which is why he spent many of his preschool days engaging in eloquent conversations with us teachers (and the children's cook) instead. The only problem was, when Arthur began telling a story, there was no stopping him. This is not an exaggeration. If Arthur started spinning his yarn during the preschool day, then Arthur became your tail, unstoppably following you until every single detail of his incredibly detailed narrative was juiced from his pomelo-sized head. Arthur never ran out of things to say. Even at the end of the day, as his tired parents attempted to lure him away from us and into his car seat, Arthur routinely felt inclined to start yet another never-ending chronicle on the doorstep. After finally locking the door, we'd naively attempt taking refuge in the staffroom, only to stop mid sigh-of-relief by the sight of Arthur's face pressed against the staffroom window, a thick fog forming around his fast-moving lips.

To make matters worse, Arthur had both a photographic memory and a doctorate in eavesdropping. This we found out the hard way.
For even when we disguised our conversations by spelling out certain words, for example, "I'm surprised Chase hasn't B I T Mr. J A X O N yet," Arthur still understood what we were saying, waited until another adult (usually a parent) walked into the room, and loudly proclaimed (I swear that boy had swallowed a microphone): "We're surprised Chase hasn't BIT JAXON yet!" with a nonchalant shrug of his tiny shoulders.

Like most young children, Arthur's dialogue was yet to develop a socially acceptable filter. As you can imagine, this little detail added constant hilarity to Arthur's non-stop chatter.

During Arthur's last year at Itty Bitties, we organised a special morning tea in honour of Father's Day. We served the fathers deformed gingerbread 'dads' made by the children who also performed a short skit from their favourite book, *Fix It Bear*.

To close, we posed the question “What do you love about your dad?” As if pricked on the buttocks with a metal pin, Arthur immediately sprung up from his seat. Like a distinguished speaker at a large conference, Arthur literally puffed out his chest, cleared his throat and lordly declared, “I like to play cheeky games. We like to wind Daddy up by putting nappies on the top of the bin!”

From my peripheral vision, I watched Arthur’s dad scratching the back of his head, a subtle blush spreading from his cheeks to his neck. Arthur wasn't finished. “My dad is good at standing up and doing a wee on the loo, because his wees just shoot right in the loo!" Thankfully, the awkward silence lasted only a second before it was broken by the children’s roar of laughter — toilet words being their number one form of entertainment.

Albert

I often wonder if it will be possible to stop my future children from becoming attached to one special toy or God forbid, a been-in-the-wars blankie. This is because, I have taught so many children who are far too dependent on their cuddlies.

Of course, as an early childhood teacher, I understand the significance of a comfort object and its ability to create links between home and preschool, but I still loathe the damn things. Take Albert for instance, newly two and faithfully devoted to Cowie — a now off-white security blanket with an attached cow's head which, put politely, had seen better days.

Albert started at Itty Bitties with Cowie hanging from his incisors, his thick drool sheening the miserable cow's head. Straightaway, it became obvious that Albert and Cowie were joined at the lips.

If Cowie was accidentally misplaced, Albert would inquire "Cowie? Cowie? Cowie? Cowie? Cowie?", without taking a single breath. When Albert's request for Cowie wasn't fulfilled within seconds, he would slap his little palms against his permanently frowning face and wail with such force that when he finally lowered his hands to retrieve

Cowie, his eyes looked as puffy and red as someone experiencing a severe allergic reaction.

Put politely, Albert and Cowie caused us teachers a lot of unnecessary stress. I recall one Friday afternoon, when Albert's mum arrived much earlier than usual to pick him up from preschool. She and Albert's dad were planning to take their little family on a spontaneous road-trip to their neighbours' luxurious lake house.

As Albert's mum gathered his belongings; backpack, drink bottle, and drawings from the day, she innocently asked: "Where's Cowie, Albert?"

The bomb was set off. There was no going back. "Cowie? Cowie? Cowie? Cowie? Where's Cowie, mum? Where's Cowie, mummy? Where's Cowie mu—"

Albert's mum lifted him up into her arms. Using her forefinger and thumb she smoothed out his frown and with a determined smile and a firm nod of the head she declared: "We'll find him, Alby."

Here was a woman on a mission. Clearly one she had prior experience in. Unlike some parents who passively wait for preschool teachers to do everything for them, Albert's mum took charge, solemnly searching everywhere from the doll's house to the mud kitchen! Young Albert, who had been transferred to my arms, simply looked on, concern seeping into his already furrowed brows. After thirty minutes, Albert's mum unsuccessfully returned, resembling someone who had just finished a thirty-minute class of hot yoga.

"I'm so sorry baby but I just can't find Cowie," she explained in defeat.

Albert's eyes widened for a millisecond before he pressed them shut and let out a deafening wail. I passed him back to his mother.

On Monday, Albert's mum told us they had to cancel their lake house escape because Albert had cried for Cowie ALL weekend — the evidence: Albert's red and swollen face. I'd love to say that was the end of dear old Cowie, but as it turned out, he was just laying low in the sandpit (understandably so, in my opinion).

Escaping to the lake house must have meant a big deal for Albert's parents because after that incident they tried everything to wean Albert off his best friend. This is when Albert started bringing an assortment of interim toys, including a tiny Thomas the Tank Engine (finding this was a hoot as you can imagine), a Golden Book, a miniscule stegosaurus (why… just why!), and a VW peace van. Albert gripped these objects like an anxious person holding onto the bar of a rollercoaster, terrified of falling to their doom at any moment. Unlike Cowie who used to hang from

Albert's lips, these provisional toys permanently occupied his hands, thus greatly limiting his movement. Albert's obsession became so bad that he simply could not function without one of his special toys in his hands. To be honest, the whole ordeal became one big home-therapy-disaster.

During this period, I had numerous nightmares where sad Albert was ghostly following me and repeatedly calling my name, followed by: "My dinosaur? My book? My van? My Thomas?" and occasionally, "Cowie?" Cue vacant mime face.

Like most toddler obsessions, one day Albert simply 'got over' his Cowie craze and all of a sudden started acting like every other 'normal' kid at our center.

Albeit, Cowie's existence remains well preserved in my persisting memories and stubborn grey hairs, the funniest being 'Disco Day' where the children dressed in their favourite outfits and we teachers just about boogied all day.

It was midday, we had 15 minutes to kill before lunch was served so we invited all of the children to come out and dance on the deck. One of the teachers set up the music whilst I handed each child two dancing ribbon rings — a bangle-sized ring with attached ribbons. The only way I managed to give Albert his ribbons was by strategically replacing them with the VW van and the Golden Book already in his tight clutch. I believe this was the first time Albert was without his new comfort objects. Before he could protest, the music started and with it, the organic unleashing of everyone's inner dancer. Both to our surprise and his, Albert started instinctually rocking his small hips. He bobbed his adorable little head and shook his illusionary large nappy-wearing bottom. He lifted his hands above his head and began admiring the way his rainbow-coloured ribbons looked in the sun's glare. Just as he was getting into the groove of using his ribbon rings, the music stopped. It was lunchtime. The children wildly threw their ribbons in my direction and raced off to wash their hands. Albert, still mesmerised, remained frozen in place, his hands still up in the air. I walked over to Albert, lowered his arms so that they were perpendicular with his body and gently took the ribbons from his hands.

"Go and wash your hands for lunch, Albert," I gently instructed him. As if in a trance, Albert slowly turned and walked in the direction of the children's bathroom, his eyes unblinking, his arms straight ahead of him, and his tiny fingers gripping the air like a baby T-rex.

Caroline

Caroline came to us under unfortunate circumstances. She was only three years old when her mother died unexpectedly in their family home. We weren't told any further details about her death, just that Caroline and her father couldn't keep living there anymore. Instead, Caroline and her father, Andy moved into the sleep-out of Andy's mother's home which happened to be around the corner from Itty Bitties.

We were expecting a sad little girl but what we got instead was pure sunshine in child-form. Caroline reminded me of a real-life Goldilocks. Her long blond hair fell in ringlets, and she had an absolutely contagious smile which I imagine had the power to warm even the iciest hearts. Caroline was full of life. She enjoyed swinging on the rope swing like Tarzan, twirling around and around like Tinkerbell, and cheekily testing the boundaries like Lilo. In my opinion, Caroline could easily slip into any Disney fairy tale. She was a dreamer who loved magical things like the invisible inhabitants of our home-made preschool fairy garden. Caroline would spend long periods of time entertaining herself at the fairy garden waiting for the fairies to appear out of their miniature glittery doors with the pearl doorknobs. Since it was an Itty Bitties rule to refrain from touching the fairy garden, as she looked on, Caroline marvelled at the fairies' tiny clothes on the small-scale clothesline, their inviting Victorian park benches and the four closed decorative doors she was certain led to the inside of their lovely homes.

Every now and then however, without warning, a violent wave of sadness washed over little Caroline. This is when Caroline cried for Eric — a soother security blanket with an attached elephant's head.

Eric the Elephant had been Caroline's comfort toy from birth. He went everywhere that Caroline did and so ended up getting either temporarily lost and/or rather mucky in the process. For this reason, Andy had explained, Caroline's mother had actually bought four Eric elephants for their precious little girl, 'just in case'.
"Oh Caroline, what's wrong? Are you okay?" I'd ask with deep concern.
"I miss my mummy," she'd reply looking down at her small hands — her voice so quiet I could hardly hear her.
"Oh Caroline, she misses you too!"
I found it so difficult to find the right words in these moments, so I'd resort to simply hugging Caroline instead. We'd hug in silence, with Caroline curled like a baby koala against my chest. We would hold each other for as long as it took for Caroline's tidal wave of sorrow to elapse.

Sometimes, she would whisper her varied thoughts into my chest: “Daddy says mummy’s gone to the moon. He says she’s not coming back but that she can actually see us from all the way up in the sky. And daddy says if I miss her, I can kiss her picture. I do that sometimes… I can talk to her in the sky because she can hear me from the moon and she’s always watching, you know.”
“That's right, Caroline,” I’d reply before reassuring her of every one of her father’s counsels.

Andy was determined to keep their life moving forward. He poured himself into his work at the local council as well as starting every form of exercise imaginable. Every morning, Caroline was dropped off at Itty Bitties by her Nana and every afternoon, she was picked up by her father looking tired but strong in his reflective running gear. Although Andy seemed calm and collected from the outside, there was no hiding his sad, often reddened eyes. “How was Caroline, today?” he'd ask forcing his weary face into a genuine smile. We’d tell him the truth: that Caroline was mostly happy with bouts of random sadness throughout the day. Andy would respond with a melancholy nod acknowledging his daughter’s all too familiar trauma.

As well as the continual support of Nana in their new life, both Caroline and Andy came to cherish the constant and steady friendship of the Millers. Bob and Sue Miller were

Nana's tender-hearted Christian neighbours who initiated the 'Monday Night Dinner' tradition where every Monday evening, they invited Caroline and Andy to their home for a comforting dinner of roast chicken.

Bob and Sue had two daughters, Isla and Skylar, who were close in age to little Caroline. These girls effortlessly became the siblings Caroline never had. Caroline loved telling her friends and teachers at preschool all about her at-home adventures with Isla and Skylar. In fact, it was clear to see Caroline's emotional cup brimming for the entire Tuesday after a Monday Night Dinner. Andy also benefited from the friendship, sharing what a relief it was not to worry about making dinner after a busy workday, as well as feeling a true sense of family again.
"It's Monday Night Dinner tonight!" Caroline would loudly announce, overflowing with excitement as soon as she stepped foot into Itty Bitties at the beginning of every week — her innocent joy was so perfectly contagious.

Caroline and Andy's pain didn't miraculously disappear, but slowly, with the help of their new village, they began handling it. What's more, the anticipation of Monday Night Dinners and the pure delight they brought to little Caroline, transformed the infamously dreaded Monday to my favourite day of the week even up to this very moment that I type her story at my desk.

Amber

Where some children had one security muzzy or comfort toy, little Amber had the entire TY collection. From Beanie Boos to Squish-a-Boos to Flippables; precious Amber owned them ALL. As Trudy and Hamish's miracle child, Amber was (understandably) unconditionally spoilt — though she was not like the stereotypical spoilt child…

Forget birthdays, every holiday (their family considered weekends holidays, too — can't say I disagree), Amber received a new TY toy.

"Look what I got!" she'd proudly share on Monday at preschool, holding up yet another unusually mixed-breed fluffy plushy (think a Bengal cat crossed with a rainbow unicorn) with its iconic sparkly TY owl eyes staring deep into our souls.

Trudy and Hamish melted each time Amber simply spoke. I imagine they liquified each time she made a request using her puppy-dog eyes — made further convincing through the magnification of her thick-rimmed pink spectacles. Hamish especially, couldn't say 'no' to his beloved only child. Above all, he had great difficulty dropping Amber off at preschool. Firstly, he always carried Amber in, even though she was four-and-a-half-years old and more than capable of walking in on her own. Secondly, he found saying goodbye excruciatingly difficult. I say excruciating because Hamish would transfer his pride and joy, who unfailingly came clutching the latest plushies, from his arms into mine, then suddenly change his mind and take her back for 'one last cuddle' (usually it is the child making this request of the parent, not the other way around). Ere long, I learnt that the 'last' cuddle was a big fat lie and in fact actually the fourth-last, sometimes fifth-last cuddle as Hamish forced us to perform the 'Amber shuffle' until my lower back nearly snapped. His goodbyes to his Amber gem became so agonising, that out of desperation, I started pretending to be busy with another child, each time Hamish finally decided to start saying goodbye. This only made the situation worse as Hamish clearly preferred to stretch out their farewell.

Little Amber, routinely sporting cat headbands and ballet tutus was well aware of her parents' unlimited love, and her own effortless powers of enchantment on all people. During the preschool day, when we least expected it, Amber would whisper in our direction: "I love you!" followed by the sweetest smile you ever saw, her eyes squinting with sweetness.

"Oh, I love you too, Amber!" we'd automatically reply. Then Amber would go back to whatever it was she was doing, probably drawing her family members in cat form, no big deal. Amber sure was clever, for her 'I love you's' were always uttered when I needed them the most. I noticed little Amber's declarations of love enchantingly soothing my negative inner thoughts, as if she was a magical creature herself. Before long, I found myself completely powerless in denying princess Amber of anything, too.

"Can I please have a book from the teacher's shelf?" (Usually off-limits to the children)

"Definitely!"

"Is it okay if I bring my fuzzies out?" (The day after our Centre Manager had sent out a community email requesting that personal toys be left at home, please and thank you.)

"Why not!"

"Can we give the baby dolls a bath?" (On a frosty winter's day)

"Sure!"

There was no denying it, I was under the Amber spell.

My favourite memory of Amber is from one of our many Itty Bitties' talent shows where the children were encouraged to perform whatever their itty-bitty hearts desired. Harvey sang and danced to Queen's iconic 'We Will Rock You'. Kyle chose a more traditional option of the children's classic: 'Incy Wincy Spider' and Elliot performed a very (with emphasis on 'very') drawn-out ‘magic’ trick. Then, it was Amber’s turn to shine. With her left cheek pressed into her shoulder and a sequin blue unicorn-cat under her right armpit, she quietly stepped up to our makeshift microphone, and took us off guard by performing immediately. Hers was an original. I imagine it was called ‘Meow’ since for the next sixty seconds, all Amber did was meow.

“Meow, meow, meow, meow, meow, meow, meow!” I’ll never forget it. You do you, Amber jewel, you do you!

Harvey

Harvey's family had moved down to our humble district from the capital (just Wellington City but think Hunger Games Capitol). All of them were tall, incredibly attractive, and their designer fashion oozed wealth and importance.

Harvey's mother, Blake, was the breadwinner of their household. She dressed in Karen Walker (New Zealand's equivalent of Dolce & Gabbana) from head to toe. Harvey's dad, Nick, was not far behind his successful spouse, regularly decked out in slim fit blazers and soft-leather boat shoes.

Harvey, just two and only knee-high, indifferently followed his parents' suit. Every morning, Harvey strutted into Itty Bitties in his skinny jeans and ankle boots like a child model walking into a photoshoot.

Similar to a bunch of groupies, we teachers would 'oooh' and 'aaah' over little Harvey's adorable outfits to which Nick, trying to appear as nonchalant as possible, would shrug and remark, "Oh, that's all his mother's doing!"

Still, I could see right through his cool. One look at his introverted smile, and it was obvious Nick secretly enjoyed the attention. It makes us sound slightly insane when I write about it now, but when the coast was clear and Harvey's parents had driven off, we'd subtly check the labels on his clothes, desperate to dress the loved little ones in our lives in the same fashion. Alas, just one internet search of said label and we'd changed our minds. Toddler Boys Stegosaurus Pants for $79.99? No, thank you.

Blake had once told me that Harvey was their 'oops' child. He had three older siblings, Margo (20), Kobe (16), and Jackson (8). Living in a household of mostly grown-ups greatly influenced young Harvey. Whilst his peers spontaneously jammed to 'Baby Shark' and 'Old MacDonald Had a Farm', Harvey rocked to alternative bands like Vampire Weekend alongside classics like Queen's 'We Will Rock You' beginning with the iconic stomp-stomp-clap, stomp-stomp-clap train.

I can distinctly remember the first time Harvey sang this song for us. It was morning group-time, and the children were waiting quietly and patiently (against our usual expectations) for my colleague to read a story when Harvey suddenly stood. He began stomp-stomp-clapping which completely amused his peers.

Then, in an intentionally deepened voice, he sang: "We will, we will, ROCK YOU!" This, he followed by the cutest air guitar ever performed.

Unlike the conventional air guitar, Harvey kept his right palm parked on his chest, whilst his extended left arm strummed ferociously, facing out! To say we were blown away by his performance is an understatement.

Harvey and his unexpected grown-up mannerisms swiftly won over our hearts. He was just too darn cute — designer dungarees or not!

Then one day, Harvey said something not so cute which literally left me open-mouthed.

Lying on the changing mat, mid nappy-change, he looked me straight in the eyes and assertively said: “Hey, you’re a bitch.”
I was stupefied. When I tactfully passed on the incident to his mother, she too was taken aback. After a sincere apology, Blake concluded, “He must have learnt that language from his eight-year-old brother Jackson’s friends.”

A week later, the children had chocolate cake for afternoon tea, courtesy of yet another 5th birthday. After handing out a miniature slice of cake to each child, Harvey took us by surprise when he put his hand up and politely asked: “Can I please have a fork?” We couldn’t believe it! Whilst his peers were shovelling the cake into their mouths using their hands like there was no tomorrow, here was a two-year-old asking for a dessert fork! How aristocratic! Of course, we obliged and gave little Harvey his fork.

All was quiet as the children devoured their afternoon treat when out of the blue and at full volume, little Harvey spoke again, this time posing his question to the room. "Excuse me, do you know what Jackson says?" he asked no one in particular.

Touched by his continuously adorable mannerisms, I replied, my face full of love and admiration: "No, Harvey, what does Jackson say?".

"Jackson says, fucking hell!"

Charlotte

Anyone who met Charlotte for the first time, automatically likened her to a porcelain doll. She was much smaller than her two-year-old peers, dainty in stature, always tastefully dressed (just like her elegant mother), with delicate features. Her emerald eyes twinkled, her nose was refined, and her thin lips were shaped into an eerie smirk permanently plastered on her translucent face. On top of that, since Charlotte had yet to start talking, her muteness simply added to her doll-like appearance.

When Charlotte started at Itty Bitties, I couldn't get over her looks. She was the most aesthetically pleasing child I had ever encountered!
However, whenever I'd compliment her perfectly plaited hairdos or high-end outfits, her mother would always respond with "Ahaha…just you wait!" leaving me feeling consistently perplexed.

As it turns out, I only had to wait one week before Charlotte began showing her true colours. One minute, Charlotte was innocently standing by the bookshelf and the next minute, Charlotte had disappeared, and the bookshelf looked as if a bomb had hit it. All of the books were thrown onto the carpet, half of them scribbled on, and the others ripped apart. Where was Charlotte?
"I saw her go into the toilet!" one child shouted. The toilet,

which was now unexpectedly flooded…

After several similar incidents, my colleague, a mother of three young children, appropriately nicknamed little Charlotte 'The Quiet Trasher'.

Then, there was the matter of transportation. There was one time I remember, when Charlotte discreetly took our student teacher's freshly made playdough containing lemon zest from the student's dying grandmother's lemon tree, and dumped the entire batch into the sandpit, deeming it unusable in an instant. This is how 'The Quiet Trasher' added 'The Transporter' to her list of names.

But little Chucky's dark habits didn't stop here (see what I did there?) As well as trashing and unfittingly transporting our resources, Charlotte derived great pleasure from pulling hair. She would quietly sneak up to a group of children, discreetly lure herself into their play, then swiftly yank out a good chunk of hair and vanish — leaving behind naught but her weeping victim(s).

"Charlie! Why did you do that?" we'd grill her. "We don't pull hair! Poor Tommy! Can you see he is hurt? He's crying! YOU made him cry."

WOW! In retrospect, I sound rather dramatic… Still, not a single reaction, zip, nada, zilch —except of course, her indefinite sinister smirk.

AJ

Anna Joy (AJ)'s parents were separated which meant many things but mainly that she was loved beyond measure. Every time AJ strutted into Itty Bitties, she arrived dressed like a little diva in an over-the-top outfit with a glittery handbag over her shoulder, and a McDonald's takeaway cup in her hands.
"It's hot chocolate," she'd announce to her fellow peers, raising her little chin and flicking her long blonde hair.

The children loved AJ. She was their Queen Bee and a Big Sister to all of them. Similar to Amber bringing a different toy into preschool each day, AJ regularly arrived with toys which I can best describe as absolutely ridiculous. There were rainbow mermaids whose tails changed colour, baby pugicorns (a pug dog with a unicorn horn), and many Christmas-themed cuddlies — most GIANT in stature. Thankfully, AJ was great at sharing and let everyone have a turn with her never-ending supply of playthings (as continuously gifted by both sets of her parents).

In addition to uninvitingly adding to our preschool resources, AJ shared a great deal of questionable information with her followers. AJ taught the children a variety of controversial TikTok dances which she'd perfected at home with her older sister — as you can imagine, I had a hard time explaining some of those moves to the parents.

Equally, AJ taught our children the 'Zombie Game' (basically a Zombie-themed variation of Tag/Chase) as inspired by watching The Walking Dead from over her dad's shoulder.

"Zombies eat brains, you know," I once heard her casually explaining to a group of her three/four-year-old peers in the playground.

After that day, I made a point to eavesdrop on AJ's conversations more often.
I swear I once heard her saying: "America is the greatest country in the world! Donald Trump is our Leader!" Where was this little girl getting this information?!

My most cherished memory of AJ (and believe me, there are many!) is her last Itty Bitties talent show performance. That day, AJ arrived at preschool looking absolutely exquisite in a 1920s style white sheath dress. I can still picture the children surrounding AJ and 'ooh'-ing and 'aah'-ing over her fabulous outfit. After Lily finished her adorable rendition of 'Mrs. Bunny', it was AJ's turn to shine. She stood up, walked to the opposite side of the preschool and grabbed a chair. She carefully positioned the chair behind our makeshift microphone stand before sitting down on it and elegantly crossing one leg over the other. "Three four...Smelly Cat, Smelly Cat, what are they feeding you? Smelly Cat, Smelly Cat, it's not your faaaault."

AJ sang her heart out, taking us teachers completely by surprise as she continued to perform the entire 'Smelly Cat' song from the iconic TV show, *Friends*. I don't know what impressed me more that day, AJ's incredible memory retention of the full song lyrics or her astonishing knowledge of adult pop culture!

Daisy

How does the child of two psychologists turn out? In short; super in touch with their emotions. Little Daisy, chocolate skinned with wild black curls, was either in a bad headspace, incredibly sour and literally barking 'No!' at anyone who spoke to her, or ecstatic on cloud nine! There was no in-between for little Daisy. She either wanted your attention or she did not.

When Daisy was bitter, she'd hide in a corner with her legs hugged into her chest. If anyone tried to approach her, she would snap at them to 'Go away!' or she'd assert herself with a simple 'No!' Sometimes it took a good thirty minutes for Daisy to regulate her emotions and escape the fire.

When Daisy was happy, she transformed into a little Frida Kahlo, producing endless self-portraits at the art table and magnanimously handing them out to her teachers. "This one's for you!" she'd beam, her brown eyes glimmering with pride.
"WOW! Thank you, Daisy! It's beautiful!"
Sixty seconds later, "This one's for you, too!"
I imagined her as a human print machine, continually spitting out art.

In either mood however, Daisy was extremely independent. From wearing her clothing and shoes to pouring her glass of water at lunchtime, Daisy was adamant on doing all the things without the assistance of an adult.

Ironically, Daisy loved to help her peers complete the very same tasks she so adamantly sought to do alone herself. Daisy was especially fond of lending a helping hand to a little toddler (who also happened to be the only child smaller in size than Daisy) called Xavier.

Xavier reminded me of a chipmunk. He was tiny in stature, he communicated in soft toddler gibberish, and he was nuts about his food — picture permanently stuffed and constantly stained cheeks.

As soon as he started at Itty Bitties, Daisy, who was only a year older than two-year-old Xavier, voluntarily took him under her wing. Daisy enjoyed doing everything for Xavier, from physically washing his hands before food to lovingly shoving his beanie on before going outside to play on a cold day.

As it turns out, there definitely is such a thing as 'too much help'. When Daisy's infatuation with serving little Xavier became borderline addictive, we had no choice but to start occasionally separating them solely for the sake of Xavier's independence. When we told Daisy that she needed to give

Xavier some space, the disappointed look on her face broke my heart to pieces. She was simply devastated.

Nonetheless, little by little, helpful Daisy learnt her limits and only came to Xavier's aid when he requested it. Like the time Xavier happened to direct a defeated look in Daisy's direction after struggling to scoop up the spaghetti Bolognese lunch with his fork, and Daisy responded by readily taking on a Mother Bird role and hand-feed him from her own…mouthful.

Anita

Baby Anita turned one the day before Covid-19 unexpectedly sent Italy into what came to be a series of seemingly never-ending stay-at-home lockdowns.

This meant that Anita and her family spent the entirety of her first year of toddlerhood homebound. By her second birthday, Anita's parents finally managed to migrate their little family back to their home country of New Zealand where, by good fortune Anita became an Itty Bitties girl.

As you'd expect, Anita's parents were particularly anxious about her starting preschool for the first time after more than a year of stay-at-home lockdowns and hotel quarantines. They were worried about how Anita would react to the other children — as the only people she had been exposed to for the majority of her life were her mother and father.

So, we trod lightly. Like most children, initially Anita found drop-offs very hard, her cries for 'mamma' lasting longer than standard. Our other barrier was that Anita's mother tongue was Italian, making our words of counsel much less effective.

In the end, Anita would calm down and allow us to wipe her big hazel eyes dry. Then, she habitually took herself to the ‘family corner’. There, she spent the rest of her preschool day completely engaged in solitary play. As if wholly oblivious to the other children, she’d routinely waddle past her noisy peers, busily muttering something or other to herself without batting an eyelid. Even if boisterous Brody or ferocious Francis tried to get her attention, Anita wouldn’t flinch. She was in a whole world of her own.

One of Anita’s favourite games to play was being ‘mum’ to all of our baby dolls. She would ‘feed’ them, read to them, clothe them, take them for a ride in the dolly stroller, pretend to wash their hands, soothe them to sleep, and my favourite, ‘video-chat’ alongside them whilst swiftly speaking into a play phone. Between her own eating and sleeping times, that’s what Anita did; she took care of the baby dolls for hours on end. During those times, I’d glance over at the family corner, and I’d see a round chocolate nugget —Anita’s straight and shiny brown hair cut into a perfect bob — sweetly swaying over the doll’s crib.

What further fascinated me about Anita’s character was her refusal to play outside. I tried every trick in the book to lure her to the playground or our garden, but she’d always respond with a subtle shake of her head. Either she was afraid of the unfamiliar outdoors, or it simply didn’t interest her. As I couldn’t be sure, I never pushed it.

After months of uninterrupted independent indoor play, Anita's parents started questioning her social skills. "Did she play with the other children today?" they began asking everyday with concerned faces.
"Not yet…" we responded again and again. "She is very chatty, though!" I'd comment. "Too bad, I can't speak much Italian."
"Oh, she's not speaking Italian!" chuckled Anita's mother.
"No?"
"No. She speaks her own language."

Then one day, 'four and three quarters' (as he loved to proudly declare himself) Finn sporadically decided to fry some meatballs next to Anita who was happily rocking her babies to sleep in the dolly stroller. All it took was one generous offering of a single meatball to be shared between her three babies, and little Anita was smitten.

After lovingly shoving the play meatball into each of her babies' plastic faces, Anita turned and faced Finn. Then, she spoke her very first words in English. "Dank you," she said, her cheeks turning rosy.

We were so delighted with little Anita's progress that we immediately messaged her parents, that she had finally not only acknowledged but also interacted with one of her peers.

"Fantastic!" responded Anita's dad straightaway. Followed by, "That's my polpetta[6]! 🧆"

[6] Meatball in Italian.

Kiaan

APPLE. BALL. SCHOOL. TRUCK. HOUSE.

Kiaan, one of the smartest children I ever taught, was writing these words (and more) at the mere age of four. Kiaan started preschool later than the average child, on the morning of his fourth birthday. Prior to coming to us, he'd received the entirety of his early childhood education from his beloved grandmother in Sri Lanka and his mother, Anu.

Anu was unlike any parent we'd ever encountered before. Even after Kiaan had attended Itty Bitties for months, without exception, every day at precisely twelve noon, Anu would call the preschool.

"Hello, it's Anu."

"Hi Anu, how are you?"

"And how is Kiaan doing today? Is he happy? Tell me, what is he playing with right now?"

Whilst my colleagues continued to find Anu's phone calls unusual, I didn't mind them so much. Anu's mannerisms reminded me of my own Persian heritage and all of the seemingly weird things my mother had done and continues to do. So, I volunteered to answer the phone every time she called.

Anu's voice was always as calm as a lake. Instead of sounding concerned, as one would expect of a calling parent, Anu's voice exuded curiosity. Before long, Anu opened up to me about her life. She told me she was a marine biologist and that her family had newly immigrated to New Zealand from Sri Lanka. Until she was eligible to work here, she had no choice but to transition to be a stay-at-home-mum for the first time. With her only child now at preschool, her husband constantly at work, without a means of transport, and her mother far away, Anu was 'so lonely and so bored'.

I loved talking about Kiaan to Anu just as much as she did for he was simply delightful. Kiaan, chocolate-skinned with an infectiously pearly white smile, ticked all the boxes of an angel child. He was well-mannered, kind, intelligent and resourceful. If he wasn't folding paper planes for his peers, helping them write their names on their artworks, or zipping up their jackets for them, Kiaan was helping us teachers with various jobs around the preschool. In fact, we often joked that Kiaan did a better job than our occasional relievers ever could.

Anu and I spoke every single day for five months before meeting face-to-face. One Friday noon, during our routine heart-to-heart, she unexpectedly invited me to visit her in their home.

I was so curious to meet my new friend that I immediately said, "Sure!"

Later, I overthought the idea until the moment I found myself waiting outside their front door.

"Hi A-nisa!" said Kiaan, who was wearing a Spiderman suit and literally bouncing up and down with excitement on their sparkly clean vinyl floor. "Please come inside!"

I followed Kiaan and the scrumptious scent of what I imagined to be turmeric fried shallots to the kitchen where Anu, dressed in a cream cotton apron over a stunning deep-blue saree, was vigorously stirring a big fat pot.

"Oh A-nisa!" she beamed, placing down her wooden spoon and showcasing yet another set of perfect pearly whites. Before I had a chance to reply, Anu had swiftly taken off her apron, rinsed her hands, and with tear-filled eyes embraced me in her thin arms.

"Thank you A-nisa! Thank you for being my lighthouse."

Acknowledgments

Writing and collating these stories into a collection would not have been made possible without the help and encouragement of four particularly wonderful people.

Delaram

Each time I finished the first draft of a story, I sent it to Delaram, my little big sister. Delaram is a mum to two toddlers: Ollie, who is written about here, and Zarrin, who, at the time of writing this book, was a dreadful sleeper. So, although her extreme sleep deprivation had made my sister indistinguishable from The Walking Dead, she still chose to read and comment on my story drafts in between baby Zarrin's catnaps instead of getting in a snooze herself. Delaram has always been my biggest fan. From faithfully saving me a place in our school cafeteria line back in Iran (aged 11 and 7), to purchase orange popsicles on a scorching summer's day, to encouraging me to follow my passion of creative writing today, and forever.

Kerry

I met Kerry on my last professional placement whilst studying to become an early childhood teacher. I remember thinking that Kerry made teaching look so effortless! One time, I saw her teaching yoga outside on the grass to a group of two-year-old children and felt completely inspired. That's the type of teacher I want to be, I thought to myself. Since then, Kerry has remained my inspiration as well as becoming my mentor, my confidante, my encourager, and one of my dearest friends. She has also taught me the importance of planning, for if I had not planned out the time to write this collection, the stories would not have so easily written themselves.

Soroosh

My dear husband, thank you for tolerating my continuous shooshing and my reading and rereading aloud. And, sorry for the many coffee cup stains on your work desk, which I claimed as my own from the early hours of 5–7am every 'writing day'. I love you dearly.

Sofia

My editor, proving Elizabeth Gilbert's theory of 'the elusive creative genius' — that we are all connected and in need of one another, and that no single work of art belongs to the individual but rather a product of myriads of inspiration. Sofia, thank you for elevating my book from what it was to what it is. Thank you for honing my craft and placing a red cherry on its top. Lastly, thank you for your patience as I went back and forth with being officially ready to submit for editing. Here's to collaborating on many more future projects.

Lastly, thank you reader, for spending your precious time reading this collection. I hope it brought a smile (or two!) to your face ☺

www.ingramcontent.com/pod-product-compliance
Lightning Source LLC
LaVergne TN
LVHW041131150826
845673LV00007B/2268

9780473581589